101 Things To Do With Ramen Noodles

Toni Patrick

16pt

Copyright Page from the Original Book

Second Digital Edition

Text © 2005 Toni Patrick
Cover and illustrations © 2023 by Gibbs Smith, Publisher
101 Things is a registered trademark of Gibbs Smith, Publisher and Stephanie Ashcraft.

All rights reserved. No part of this book may be reproduced by any means whatsoever without written permission from the publisher, except brief portions quoted for purpose of review.

First Gibbs Smith edition published in 2005
Second Gibbs Smith edition published May 2023

Published by
Gibbs Smith, Publisher
P.O. Box 667
Layton, Utah 84041

1.800.835.4993 orders
www.gibbs-smith.com

Designed by Ryan Thomann and Renee Bond

Library of Congress has cataloged the first edition as follows:
Patrick, Toni.
101 things to do with ramen noodles / Toni Patrick.—1st ed.
p. cm.

1. Cookery (Pasta) 2. Noodles. I. Title: One hundred one things to do with ramen noodles. II. Title: One hundred and one things to do with ramen noodles. III. Title.
TX809.M17P376 2005
641.8'22—dc22
2005002259

TABLE OF CONTENTS

Helpful Hints	iv
1–11: SOUPS	1
1: Minestrone	1
2: Egg Drop Soup	3
3: Beefed-Up Noodles	4
4: Chicken Consommé and Noodles	5
5: Creamy Chicken Noodle Soup	6
6: Creamy Mushroom Soup	7
7: Tomato Noodle Soup	8
8: Vegetable Beef Noodle Soup	9
9: Summer Garden Soup	10
10: Southwest Vegetable Soup	11
11: Asian-Inspired Beef Noodle Soup	12
12–22: SALADS	14
12: Spring Salad	14
13: Summer Picnic Salad	16
14: Antipasto Salad	17
15: Zucchini Salad	18
16: Taco Salad	19
17: Three-Bean Salad	20
18: Pasta Salad	21
19: Water Chestnut Ramen Salad	22
20: Chicken Salad with Almonds and Sesame Seeds	23
21: Fruity Ramen Salad	25
22: Sweet-and-Sour Salad	27
23–39: BEEF	28
23: Beef Rameno	28
24: Creamy Beef and Broccoli Noodles	29
25: Beef Provençal	30
26: Marinated Beef	32
27: Cheddar and Beef Casserole	33
28: Beef and Broccoli Stir-Fry	34

29: Ramen Burgers	35
30: Cheeseburger Ramen	36
31: Japanese-Style Beef and Noodles	37
32: Beefy Mushroom Noodles	39
33: Vegetable Beef Noodles	40
34: Beef 'n' Potato Noodles	41
35: Beefy Chili Noodles	42
36: Spicy Beef Noodles	43
37: Spicy Meat-and-Cheese Roll	44
38: Country Vegetable Beef	45
39: Beefy Noodles with Gravy	46
40–58: CHICKEN	47
40: Creamy Chicken and Broccoli	47
41: Spicy Chicken	48
42: Cheesy Chicken Divan	49
43: Easy Chicken Allemande	51
44: Chicken "Lo Mein"	53
45: Chicken Hollandaise	54
46: Chicken Ramen Velouté	55
47: Chicken Curry	56
48: Chicken with Creamy Herb Sauce	57
49: Creamy Chicken Noodles	59
50: Chicken with Mushrooms	60
51: Chicken Alfredo	61
52: Fajita-Inspired Ramen	62
53: Italian Chicken	63
54: Fiesta Chicken	64
55: Cheesy Chicken Casserole	65
56: Chicken 'n' Asparagus	66
57: Chinese-Style Ramen	67
58: Chicken Milano	68
59–67: PORK	69
59: All-American Ramen	69
60: Ham and Cheese Ramen Omelets	70

61: Cheesy Bacon Noodles	71
62: Brats 'n' Noodles	72
63: Pork and Peppers	73
64: Pork Chop Ramen	75
65: Hungarian-Style Skillet Meal	76
66: Lean Pork Steak	77
67: Tropical Ramen	78
68–74: SEAFOOD	79
68: Cheesy Tuna Ramen	79
69: Tuna Noodle Casserole	80
70: Twice-Baked Tuna Casserole	81
71: Creamy Mushroom Shrimp Ramen	82
72: Cheesy Salmon Noodles	83
73: Shrimp Ramen	84
74: Garlic Shrimp 'n' Veggies	85
75–92: FAMILY FAVORITES	86
75: Ramen Nachos	86
76: Garlic Noodle Sauté	87
77: Creamy Alfredo Noodles	88
78: Crunchy, Cheesy Casserole	89
79: Pizza Pasta	90
80: Lasagna	91
81: Meaty Spaghetti	92
82: Primavera Pasta	93
83: Parmesan Noodles	94
84: Cheesy Noodles	95
85: Cheesy Ranch Ramen	96
86: Buttery Chive Noodles	97
87: Onion Noodles	98
88: Ramen Trail Mix	99
89: Ramen Haystacks	100
90: Crunchy Chocolate-Coconut Bars	101
91: Peach Treats	102
92: Maple and Brown Sugar Ramenmeal	103

93–101: VEGETABLE ENTRÉES 104
    93: Broccoli-Cauliflower Ramen 104
    94: Cheesy Vegetable Ramen 105
    95: Hollandaise Vegetable Noodles 106
    96: Veggie Sauté 107
    97: Chinese-Style Fried Noodles 108
    98: Tomato Sauté 109
    99: Garlic and Cilantro Noodles 110
    100: Creamy Corn and Cheese Noodles 111
    101: Soy Sauce Veggie Noodles 112
About the Author 116

i

This book is dedicated to my mother. If it weren't for her threatening to steal my idea and do the book herself, I wouldn't have done it.
I love you, Mom.

iii

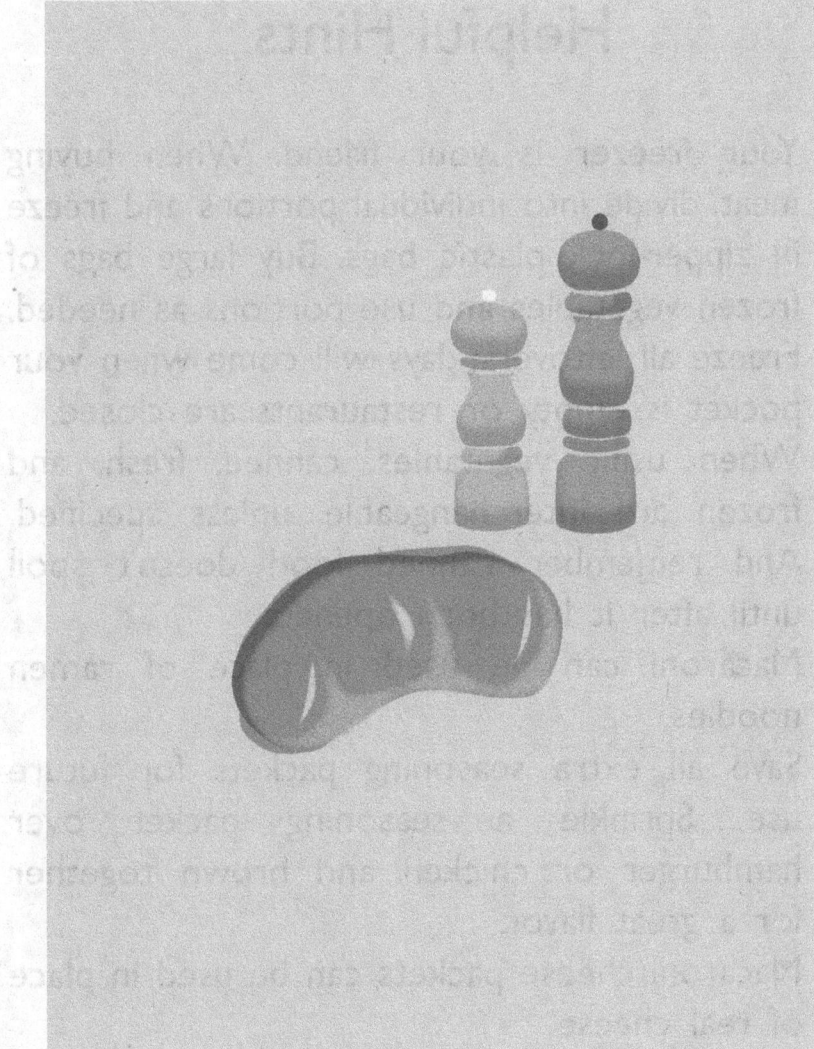

Helpful Hints

- Your freezer is your friend. When buying meat, divide into individual portions and freeze in zipper-lock plastic bags. Buy large bags of frozen vegetables and use portions as needed. Freeze all leftovers; days will come when your pocket is empty or restaurants are closed.
- When using vegetables, canned, fresh, and frozen are interchangeable, unless specified. And remember, canned food doesn't spoil until after it has been opened.
- Macaroni can be used in place of ramen noodles.
- Save all extra seasoning packets for future use. Sprinkle a seasoning packet over hamburger or chicken and brown together for a great flavor.
- Macaroni cheese packets can be used in place of real cheese.
- Two tablespoons dehydrated minced or chopped onion is equal to 1/4 cup fresh minced onion.
- Salt lovers beware. Before adding extra salt, taste your food. Seasoning packets are always salty.
- To cook noodles, follow the directions on the package unless recipe says otherwise.

- Add more or less of any ingredient to your own liking. Be creative and enjoy yourself.
- Low-fat or light soups, sour cream, and cream cheese can be substituted if you prefer.

SOUPS

Minestrone

MAKES 2 SERVINGS

1 package ramen noodles, any flavor
1 can (10.75 ounces) condensed tomato soup
8 ounces cooked spicy smoked sausage, thinly sliced
1/4 cup cooked sliced celery
1/4 cup cooked sliced carrots
1/4 cup peas
1/2 cup green beans
1/2 cup canned kidney beans, drained and rinsed
salt and pepper, to taste

Cook noodles in water according to package directions. Do not drain. Add soup, sausage, and vegetables. Simmer 5–10 minutes, or until vegetables are tender. Add more water by tablespoon if soup is too thick. Season with salt and pepper.

Egg Drop Soup

MAKES 2 SERVINGS

2 cups water
1 package chicken ramen noodles, with seasoning packet
2 eggs, beaten
1/4 cup diced onion
1/4 cup diced celery
1/4 cup diced green bell pepper

In a saucepan, bring water to boiling and add seasoning packet, eggs, and vegetables. Stir constantly until eggs look done. Simmer 5 minutes. Add noodles and cook 3–5 minutes more, or until noodles are tender.

Beefed-Up Noodles

MAKES 2 SERVINGS

2 cups water
1/8 cup diced onion
1/8 cup sliced carrots
1/8 cup diced celery
1 sprig parsley
1 small bay leaf
1/8 teaspoon thyme leaves
1 package beef ramen noodles, with seasoning packet

In a saucepan, heat all ingredients except noodles and seasoning packet to boiling. Add seasoning packet. Reduce heat and simmer 30 minutes. Strain liquid into a separate container. Add noodles to liquid and cook 3 minutes, or until noodles are done.

Chicken Consommé and Noodles

MAKES 2 SERVINGS

**2 cups water
1/8 cup diced onion
1/8 cup sliced carrots
1/8 cup diced celery
1 sprig parsley
1 small bay leaf
1/8 teaspoon thyme leaves
1 package chicken ramen noodles, with seasoning packet**

In a saucepan, heat all ingredients except noodles and seasoning packet to boiling. Add seasoning packet. Reduce heat and simmer 30 minutes. Strain liquid into a separate container. Add noodles to liquid and cook 3 minutes, or until noodles are done.

Creamy Chicken Noodle Soup

MAKES 2 SERVINGS

1 package chicken ramen noodles, with seasoning packet
1 can (10.75 ounces) condensed cream of chicken soup
1/2 cup diced onion
1/2 cup sliced carrots
1/2 cup sliced celery

Cook noodles in water according to package directions and drain.

Prepare soup as directed on can. Add seasoning packet and vegetables to soup. Cook over medium heat 5–10 minutes, or until vegetables are tender. Add noodles and simmer 2–3 minutes more.

Creamy Mushroom Soup

MAKES 2 SERVINGS

1 package ramen noodles, any flavor
1 can (10.75 ounces) condensed cream of mushroom soup
1 cup sliced fresh mushrooms
salt and pepper, to taste

    Cook noodles in water according to package directions and drain.
    Prepare soup as directed on can. Mix noodles and soup together. Add mushrooms and simmer 5 minutes. Season with salt and pepper.

Tomato Noodle Soup

MAKES 2 SERVINGS

**1 package ramen noodles, any flavor
1 can (10.75 ounces) condensed tomato soup**

Cook noodles in water according to package directions. Do not drain. Add soup. Simmer 5 minutes, stirring occasionally.

Vegetable Beef Noodle Soup

MAKES 2–4 SERVINGS

3/4 pound ground beef
1 cup chopped tomatoes
1/2 cup chopped carrots
1/2 cup chopped celery
4 cups water
2 packages beef ramen noodles, with seasoning packets

In a frying pan, brown and drain beef. Add vegetables, water, and seasoning packets. Bring to a boil and simmer 20 minutes. Add noodles and cook 3 minutes more, or until noodles are done.

Summer Garden Soup

MAKES 2–4 SERVINGS

1/2 cup chopped onion
1 cup julienned zucchini
1/2 cup chopped carrots
1/4 cup butter or margarine
1 teaspoon basil
2 packages beef ramen noodles, with seasoning packets
4 cups water
1 cup green beans
1 cup chopped tomatoes

In a frying pan, cook onion, zucchini, and carrots in butter and basil over medium heat until vegetables are tender.

In a saucepan, combine cooked vegetables, noodles, water, green beans, tomatoes, and seasoning packets. Heat to boiling and simmer 5 minutes.

Southwest Vegetable Soup

MAKES 2 SERVINGS

1 can (10.75 ounces) condensed tomato soup
1 cup water
1 can (10.75 ounces) enchilada sauce
1/2 cup corn
1/2 cup green beans
1/2 cup canned kidney beans, drained and rinsed
1/2 cup salsa
1/2 cup chopped cooked chicken
1 package ramen noodles, any flavor, crumbled
tortilla chips
Monterey Jack cheese, grated

In a soup pot, combine tomato soup, water, and enchilada sauce. Cook over medium heat until hot. Add vegetables, salsa, and chicken. Simmer 15 minutes. Add crumbled noodles and simmer 3–5 minutes more. Serve topped with chips and cheese.

11

Asian-Inspired Beef Noodle Soup

MAKES 4–6 SERVINGS

1 pound ground beef, browned and drained
1 medium onion, chopped
1 tablespoon minced garlic
1 teaspoon ground ginger
5 cups water
1 medium head bok choy
2 packages beef ramen noodles, with seasoning packets
1 1/2 teaspoons canola oil
2 tablespoons soy sauce

In a 4-quart soup pot, combine cooked beef, onion, garlic, ginger, and water, and bring to a boil. Stir in bok choy. Simmer over medium heat 3 minutes. Break noodles in half and stir into soup. Simmer 3–5 minutes more, or until noodles are done. Stir in seasoning packets, oil, and soy sauce.

To prepare bok choy for use, rinse with cold water, cut off the very bottom of the stems and discard. Cut remaining bok choy into bite-size pieces.

12–22

SALADS

12

Spring Salad

MAKES 2–4 SERVINGS

2 packages chicken ramen noodles, with seasoning packets
2 teaspoons sesame oil
3 tablespoons lemon juice
1/3 cup vegetable oil
2 teaspoons sugar
1 cup halved red and/or green seedless grapes
1/2 cup diced red and/or green apple
1/2 cup diced pineapple chunks
3 tablespoons chopped green onion
8 ounces smoked turkey breast, cut into strips
1/4 cup walnut pieces

Cook noodles in water according to package directions and drain. Rinse with cold water. Add sesame oil and refrigerate.

For dressing, combine lemon juice, vegetable oil, seasoning packets, and sugar. Pour over noodles. Then add grapes, apple, pineapple, onion, turkey, and walnut pieces. Toss to coat.

13

Summer Picnic Salad

MAKES 2 SERVINGS

1 package ramen noodles, any flavor, broken up
1/4 cup alfalfa sprouts
1/2 cup peas
French dressing

Cook noodles in water according to package directions and drain. Top with alfalfa sprouts and peas. Mix with desired amount of dressing.

14

Antipasto Salad

MAKES 2–4 SERVINGS

2 packages ramen noodles, any flavor
3/4 cup cubed pepperoni
1/2 cup sliced black olives
1/4 cup sliced onion
Italian dressing

Cook noodles in water according to package directions and drain. Add pepperoni, olives, and onion. Drizzle desired amount of dressing over top and toss to coat.

15

Zucchini Salad

MAKES 2 SERVINGS

1 package ramen noodles, any flavor
1/2 cup chopped zucchini
1/2 cup chopped carrots
1/8 cup sliced olives
1 teaspoon Dijon mustard
1/2 teaspoon basil
1/4 teaspoon oregano
1/4 teaspoon garlic powder
2 tablespoons vinegar

Cook noodles in water according to package directions and drain. Add vegetables to noodles. In a small bowl, mix together mustard, spices, and vinegar. Add to noodle mixture and toss to coat.

16

Taco Salad

MAKES 2–4 SERVINGS

2 packages beef ramen noodles, with seasoning packets
1 pound ground beef, browned and drained
1 large tomato, chopped
3/4 cup chopped onion
2 cups grated cheddar cheese
Thousand Island dressing or salsa

Cook noodles in water according to package directions and drain.

In a large bowl, stir 1 seasoning packet into cooked beef. Add tomato, onion, and cheese. Spoon mixture over warm noodles and drizzle with dressing or salsa.

17

Three-Bean Salad

MAKES 2 SERVINGS

1 package ramen noodles, any flavor
1/2 cup green beans
1/2 cup canned kidney beans, drained and rinsed
1/2 cup canned lima beans, drained and rinsed
1/4 cup Italian dressing
salt and pepper, to taste

Cook noodles in water according to package directions and drain. Add beans and stir in dressing. Season with salt and pepper.

18

Pasta Salad

MAKES 2 SERVINGS

1 package ramen noodles, any flavor, with seasoning packet
1/2 cup mayonnaise
1 tablespoon mustard
1 1/2 teaspoons honey
1 celery stalk, chopped
1/4 cup cubed cheddar cheese
2 hard-boiled eggs, chopped

Cook noodles in water according to package directions and drain. In a large bowl, mix mayonnaise, mustard, and honey with 1/2 of the seasoning packet. Add noodles, celery, cheese, and eggs. Toss gently to coat.

19

Water Chestnut Ramen Salad

MAKES 4–6 SERVINGS

4 packages chicken ramen noodles, with seasoning packets
1 cup diced celery
1 can (8 ounces) sliced water chestnuts, drained
1 cup chopped red onion
1 cup diced green bell pepper
1 cup peas
1 cup mayonnaise

    Break each package of noodles into 4 pieces. Cook noodles in water according to package directions, then drain and rinse with cold water.
    In a large bowl, stir noodles, celery, water chestnuts, onion, pepper, and peas together. In a medium bowl, combine mayonnaise and 3 seasoning packets. Fold mayonnaise mixture into salad. Cover and refrigerate at least 1 hour before serving.

20

Chicken Salad with Almonds and Sesame Seeds

MAKES 2–4 SERVINGS

1 package ramen noodles, any flavor
1 teaspoon vinegar
1/2 cup oil
3 teaspoons seasoned salt
1/2 teaspoon pepper
3 tablespoons sugar
4 cups shredded cooked chicken breast
3 to 6 green onions, sliced
3/4 cup sliced celery
1/4 cup sesame seeds
1 cup slivered almonds
1/2 head lettuce, torn or shredded

Cook noodles in water for 1 minute and drain.

In a large bowl, mix vinegar, oil, salt, pepper, and sugar. Add chicken, onions, celery, and sesame seeds. Add prepared noodles and roasted almonds. Add lettuce just before serving and toss.

For more flavor, roast the almonds in a 350 degree oven for about 10 minutes until lightly browned, stirring every couple of minutes to avoid burning.

21

Fruity Ramen Salad

MAKES 2 SERVINGS

Dressing:
1/2 teaspoon salt
dash pepper
1 teaspoon vegetable oil
1 tablespoon chopped parsley
2 tablespoons sugar
2 tablespoons vinegar
dash vinegar hot sauce, such as Tabasco

Salad:
1 package ramen noodles, any flavor
1/2 cup slivered almonds
2 tablespoons sugar
1 cup diced cooked ham
1 can (10 ounces) mandarin oranges, drained

In a small bowl, combine dressing ingredients and set aside.

Cook noodles in water according to package directions, then drain and rinse with cold water.

In a frying pan, lightly brown almonds and sugar over medium heat, stirring constantly so almonds are coated in sugar.

In a large bowl, mix ham, oranges, and noodles. Add dressing and toss to coat. Just before serving, add almonds and toss again.

22

Sweet-and-Sour Salad

MAKES 6–8 SERVINGS

1 cup canola or olive oil
1/2 cup sugar
1/2 cup apple cider vinegar
1 tablespoon soy sauce
1/2 cup butter
1 cup chopped walnuts
1 package ramen noodles, any flavor, crushed
1 head romaine lettuce
4 cups chopped fresh broccoli
1/2 cup chopped green onions

In a medium bowl, combine oil, sugar, vinegar, and soy sauce together. Cover and refrigerate overnight.

In a saucepan, melt butter over medium heat. Stir walnuts and noodles into butter. Stir until heated.

Tear lettuce into bite-size pieces and place in a large bowl. Add broccoli and onions. Pour dressing over top and toss to coat. Sprinkle walnut-ramen mixture over salad.

BEEF

23

Beef Rameno

MAKES 2 SERVINGS

1/2 pound beef strips
2 cups sour cream
1 tablespoon chopped chives
1 teaspoon salt
1/8 teaspoon pepper
1 garlic clove, crushed
1/2 cup grated Parmesan cheese, divided
1 packages ramen noodles, any flavor
2 tablespoons butter or margarine

In a frying pan, brown beef until done. Add sour cream, spices, and 1/4 cup Parmesan, and simmer over low heat.

Cook noodles in water according to package directions and drain. Stir butter into warm noodles until melted. Fold in beef mixture. Sprinkle with remaining 1/4 cup cheese.

24

Creamy Beef and Broccoli Noodles

MAKES 2 SERVINGS

3/4 pound beef sirloin, cubed
1/2 teaspoon garlic powder
1 onion, cut into wedges
2 cups broccoli pieces
1 can (10.75 ounces) condensed cream of broccoli soup
1/4 cup water
1 tablespoon soy sauce
2 packages beef ramen noodles, with seasoning packets

In a frying pan, brown beef with garlic powder until done. Stir in onion and broccoli. Cook over medium heat until vegetables are tender. Add soup, water, and soy sauce. Simmer 10 minutes.

Cook noodles in water according to package directions and drain. Add seasoning packets. Serve beef mixture over warm noodles.

Beef Provençal

MAKES 2 SERVINGS

1 pound beef strips
1 package beef ramen noodles, with seasoning packet
1 cup water
2 tablespoons butter or margarine
1 onion, sliced
2 tablespoons our
1 tomato, chopped
1 can (4 ounces) sliced mushrooms, drained
1 teaspoon garlic powder

In a frying pan, brown beef until done.

In a small bowl, mix together seasoning packet and water.

In a saucepan, heat butter until golden brown. Add onion and cook until tender, then discard onion. Stir in flour, over low heat, until brown. Remove from heat. Add water mixture and heat to boiling, stirring constantly for 1 minute. Gently stir in tomato, mushrooms, and garlic powder.

Cook noodles in water according to package directions and drain.

Top warm noodles with beef and sauce.

26

Marinated Beef

MAKES 2 SERVINGS

3/4 pound beef strips
1 package beef ramen noodles, with seasoning packet
1/2 cup water
2 tablespoons oil
1/4 cup sliced green onion
1 tablespoon butter or margarine
1 can (14.5 ounces) diced tomatoes, drained

In a large bowl, marinate beef in seasoning packet, water, and oil for 30 minutes. In a frying pan, cook beef in marinade until done. Add onion and butter, and sauté 5 minutes.

Cook noodles in water according to package directions and drain. Add tomatoes and cooked noodles to beef mixture. Simmer 5–10 minutes, or until heated through.

27

Cheddar and Beef Casserole

MAKES 2–4 SERVINGS

2 packages beef ramen noodles, with seasoning packets
1 pound ground beef
1/2 cup sliced celery
1/4 cup chopped green bell pepper
1/2 cup chopped onion
3 cups grated cheddar cheese
2 cups corn
1 can (6 ounces) tomato paste
1/2 cup water

Preheat oven to 350 degrees.

Cook noodles in water according to package directions; drain and set aside.

In a frying pan, brown beef with celery, pepper, and onion. Set aside.

In a 2-quart casserole dish, mix remaining ingredients with 1 seasoning packet. Add beef mixture and noodles and toss to coat. Bake 15–20 minutes.

28

Beef and Broccoli Stir-Fry

MAKES 2–4 SERVINGS

1 pound beef strips
1 tablespoon oil
2 packages beef ramen noodles, with seasoning packets
2 cups broccoli pieces
1 cup green onions, cut into strips
2 tablespoons soy sauce
1/4 teaspoon crushed red pepper

In a frying pan, brown and drain beef. Add oil, 1 seasoning packet, broccoli, and onions. Stir-fry 5 minutes. Add soy sauce and red pepper. Simmer 5 minutes more.

Cook noodles in water according to package directions and drain. Serve beef mixture over warm noodles.

29

Ramen Burgers

MAKES 4 HAMBURGERS

1 package beef ramen noodles, with seasoning packet
1 pound ground beef
1 egg
4 hamburger buns

Cook noodles in water 1 1/2 minutes and drain. Add beef, egg, and 1/2 of the seasoning packet. Mix well and form into four patties. Grill or cook 5 minutes per side, or until desired doneness.

Serve these with your favorite hamburger fixings, including lettuce, tomato, ketchup, and mustard.

30

Cheeseburger Ramen

MAKES 2 SERVINGS

1/2 pound ground beef
1 package beef ramen noodles, with seasoning packet
1 cup grated cheddar cheese
1 tomato, diced, optional

In a frying pan, brown and drain beef. Season to taste with 1/2 of the seasoning packet.
Cook noodles in water according to package directions and drain. Add beef and cheese to noodles and stir until cheese is melted. Add tomatoes, if desired.

31

Japanese-Style Beef and Noodles

MAKES 2–4 SERVINGS

2 packages beef ramen noodles, with seasoning packets
1/2 cup water
1 pound beef strips
2 tablespoons oil
2 tablespoons sugar
1/2 cup soy sauce
1 can (4 ounces) sliced mushrooms, drained
1/2 cup sliced green onions
1 cup sliced onion
1 celery stalk, sliced
1 can (8 ounces) bamboo shoots
3 cups fresh spinach

In a small bowl, mix together 1/2 of 1 seasoning packet and water.

In a frying pan, brown beef in oil until done, then push to one side of the pan. Stir in water mixture, sugar, and soy sauce. Add mushrooms, green onion, onion, celery, bamboo shoots, and spinach and cook until tender. Cover and simmer 5 minutes. Stir together.

Cook noodles in water according to package directions and drain. Add remaining 1 1/2 seasoning packets. Serve beef mixture over warm noodles.

32

Beefy Mushroom Noodles

MAKES 2–4 SERVINGS

2 packages beef ramen noodles, with seasoning packets
2 cups water
1 1/2 pounds beef strips
1/4 cup butter or margarine
2 cans (4 ounces each) sliced mushrooms, drained
1/4 cup our
Worcestershire sauce, to taste

Cook noodles in water according to package directions and drain.

In a medium bowl, mix together seasoning packets and water.

In a frying pan, brown and drain beef.

In a small saucepan, melt butter over low heat. Stir in mushrooms and brown slowly. Add our and cook, stirring, until deep brown. Add water mixture. Heat to boiling and stir 1 minute. Add Worcestershire sauce. Top warm noodles with beef and sauce.

33

Vegetable Beef Noodles

MAKES 2 SERVINGS

**1/2 pound ground beef
1 can (8 ounces) tomato sauce
2 cups frozen mixed vegetables
1 package beef ramen noodles, with seasoning packet**

In a frying pan, brown and drain beef. Add tomato sauce, vegetables, and seasoning packet to cooked beef. Simmer 10 minutes, or until vegetables are tender.

Cook noodles in water according to package directions and drain. Add noodles to beef mixture and simmer 2–3 minutes.

34

Beef 'n' Potato Noodles

MAKES 2–4 SERVINGS

1 pound ground beef
2 packages beef ramen noodles, with seasoning packets
2 cups cubed potatoes
2 cups diced tomatoes

In a frying pan, brown beef with seasoning packets until done. Add potatoes and cook until tender.

Cook noodles in water according to package directions and drain. Stir in tomatoes, then add noodles and tomatoes to beef mixture and simmer 5 minutes.

Beefy Chili Noodles

MAKES 2–4 SERVINGS

1 pound ground beef
2 packages beef ramen noodles, with seasoning packets
2 cans (4 ounces each) sliced mushrooms, drained
1/2 cup chopped onion
1/2 cup chopped tomato
1 can (15 ounces) kidney beans, drained and rinsed
1/4 teaspoon chili powder
1 cup water

In a frying pan, brown and drain beef. Add noodles, mushrooms, onion, tomato, kidney beans, chili powder, water, and 1 seasoning packet. Simmer 10 minutes or until noodles are done.

36

Spicy Beef Noodles

MAKES 2–4 SERVINGS

2 packages ramen noodles, any flavor, with seasoning packets
1/2 pound ground beef
1/2 pound ground spicy sausage
1/2 cup diced onion
3/4 cup diced green bell pepper
3/4 cup salsa

Cook noodles in water according to package directions; drain and set aside.

In a frying pan, brown beef and sausage together then drain. Add onion, pepper, and salsa. Cook until vegetables are tender. Add noodles and simmer 2–3 minutes.

Spicy Meat-and-Cheese Roll

MAKES 2–4 SERVINGS

1 pound ground beef
1 package beef ramen noodles, crushed
1 cup grated cheddar cheese
1/2 cup salsa

Preheat oven to 350 degrees.
Flatten beef into a 1/2-inch-thick rectangle in a baking dish. Sprinkle uncooked noodles over beef. Top with a layer of cheese. Roll from one end to the other and pinch ends to prevent cheese from melting to the outside. Transfer to a loaf pan, then top with salsa.
Bake 30 minutes. Top with more salsa before serving, if desired.

38

Country Vegetable Beef

MAKES 2–4 SERVINGS

2 cups water
2 tablespoons cornstarch
2 packages beef ramen noodles, with seasoning packets
1 pound ground beef
4 cups frozen mixed vegetables

In a small saucepan, mix water, cornstarch, and seasoning packets. Stir constantly over low heat until mixture thickens.

In a frying pan, brown and drain beef. Add vegetables and cook until tender. Add gravy and stir.

Cook noodles in water according to package directions and drain. Serve gravy over warm noodles.

39

Beefy Noodles with Gravy

MAKES 2 SERVINGS

1 pound beef strips
1 package beef ramen noodles, with seasoning packet
1 envelope brown gravy mix

In a frying pan, brown beef until done.

Cook noodles in water according to package directions; drain and set aside.

In a saucepan, prepare gravy according to package directions. Top warm noodles with beef and gravy.

CHICKEN

40

Creamy Chicken and Broccoli

MAKES 2–4 SERVINGS

3 boneless, skinless chicken breasts, cut into strips
2 cups chopped fresh or frozen broccoli
2 cans (10.75 ounces each) condensed cream of mushroom soup
2 packages chicken ramen noodles, with seasoning packets

In a frying pan, brown chicken until done. Add broccoli and soup to chicken. Cook over medium heat until broccoli is tender. Add 1/2 of 1 seasoning packet, or to taste.

Cook noodles in water according to package directions and drain. Serve chicken and broccoli mixture over warm noodles.

41

Spicy Chicken

MAKES 2–4 SERVINGS

3 boneless, skinless chicken breasts, cut into strips
3/4 teaspoon garlic powder
1 can (14.5 ounces) diced tomatoes with green chilies, drained
1 cup chopped green bell peppers
2 cups water
2 packages chicken ramen noodles, with seasoning packets

In a frying pan, brown chicken until done. Add garlic powder, tomatoes and chilies, peppers, water, and seasoning packets. Simmer 10 minutes. Add noodles and cook 3–5 minutes more.

Cheesy Chicken Divan

MAKES 2–4 SERVINGS

2 cups fresh broccoli pieces
2 to 4 boneless, skinless chicken breasts, cut into chunks
2 packages chicken ramen noodles
1 can (10.75 ounces) condensed cream of chicken soup
3/4 cup mayonnaise
1 teaspoon mild curry powder
salt and pepper, to taste
1 cup grated cheddar cheese

Preheat oven to 350 degrees.

Place broccoli in a saucepan and cover with water. Cook over medium heat until broccoli is tender. Drain and spread in a lightly greased 9x9-inch casserole dish.

In a frying pan, brown chicken until done. Spread chicken over broccoli.

Cook noodles in water according to package directions and drain. Spread noodles over broccoli and chicken.

Mix together soup, mayonnaise, curry powder, salt, and pepper. Spoon mixture over broccoli, chicken, and noodles; sprinkle with cheese and bake 30 minutes.

Easy Chicken Allemande

MAKES 2 SERVINGS

2 boneless, skinless chicken breasts, cut into chunks
2 packages chicken ramen noodles, with seasoning packets
1 cup water
2 tablespoons our
salt and pepper, to taste
1/8 teaspoon nutmeg
1 egg yolk
2 tablespoons butter or margarine, melted
2 tablespoons heavy cream
1 teaspoon lemon juice

In a frying pan, brown chicken until done.

Cook noodles in water according to package directions and drain.

In a small bowl, mix together water and 1 seasoning packet.

In a saucepan, mix our, salt, pepper, and nutmeg together. Beat egg yolk into water mixture, and then stir into our mixture. Heat to boiling and boil 1 minute, stirring constantly.

Remove from heat. Stir in butter, cream, and lemon juice. Add chicken and simmer 2–3 minutes. Top warm noodles with chicken and sauce.

44

Chicken "Lo Mein"

MAKES 2 SERVINGS

1 tablespoon oil
1 tablespoon soy sauce
1 package chicken ramen noodles, with seasoning packet
1 pound boneless, skinless chicken breasts, cut into strips
1/2 cup sliced onion
1/2 cup chopped green bell pepper
1/4 cup chopped carrot

In a frying pan, mix oil, soy sauce, and 1/2 of the seasoning packet. Add chicken and brown until done. Add vegetables to chicken, and cook until tender.

Cook noodles in water according to package directions and drain. Add noodles to chicken and vegetables and cook over medium heat 3 minutes, stirring constantly.

45

Chicken Hollandaise

MAKES 2–4 SERVINGS

2 to 4 boneless, skinless chicken breasts, cut into chunks
2 packages chicken ramen noodles, with seasoning packets
4 egg yolks
6 tablespoons lemon juice
1 cup butter or margarine

In a frying pan, brown chicken until done. Season with 1/2 of 1 seasoning packet, or to taste.

In a small saucepan, whisk egg yolks and lemon juice briskly with a fork. Add 1/2 cup butter and stir over low heat until melted. Add remaining butter, stirring briskly until butter melts and sauce thickens.

Cook noodles in water according to package directions and drain. Top warm noodles with chicken and sauce.

46

Chicken Ramen Velouté

MAKES 2 SERVINGS

1 pound boneless, skinless chicken breasts, cut into chunks
1 cup water
1 package chicken ramen noodles, with seasoning packet
2 tablespoons butter or margarine
2 tablespoons our
1/8 teaspoon nutmeg

In a frying pan, brown chicken until done.

In a small bowl, mix together water and 1 seasoning packet.

In a saucepan, melt butter over low heat. Mix in our, stirring until smooth and bubbly. Remove from heat. Stir in water mixture and nutmeg. Heat to boiling, stirring 1 minute. Add chicken and simmer over low heat until warmed through.

Cook noodles in water according to package directions and drain. Top warm noodles with chicken and sauce.

Chicken Curry

MAKES 2 SERVINGS

2 boneless, skinless chicken breasts
1/4 cup butter or margarine
1/4 cup our
1/2 teaspoon curry powder
2 packages chicken ramen noodles, with seasoning packets
2 cups milk

In a frying pan, brown chicken until done. Set aside.

In a small saucepan, melt butter. Stir in flour, curry powder, and 1 seasoning packet. Cook on low heat, stirring until smooth and bubbly. Add milk and heat to boiling, stirring 1 minute. Add chicken and simmer over low heat until warmed through.

Cook noodles in water according to package directions and drain. Top warm noodles with chicken and sauce.

48

Chicken with Creamy Herb Sauce

MAKES 2 SERVINGS

2 boneless, skinless chicken breasts, cut into chunks
1 package chicken ramen noodles, with seasoning packet
1 cup water
2 tablespoons butter or margarine
2 tablespoons our
2 tablespoons chopped onion
1 tablespoon vinegar
1 tablespoon chopped parsley
1/4 teaspoon tarragon leaves
1/4 teaspoon thyme leaves

In a frying pan, brown chicken until done. Cook noodles in water according to package directions; drain and set aside.

In a small bowl, mix together water and 1 seasoning packet.

In a small saucepan, heat butter over low heat until golden brown. Blend in our, stirring until deep brown. Remove from heat. Add water mixture, onion, vinegar, and herbs, and heat to boiling, stirring 1 minute. Top warm noodles with chicken and sauce.

49

Creamy Chicken Noodles

MAKES 2 SERVINGS

1 package chicken ramen noodles, with seasoning packet
1 can (10.75 ounces) condensed cream of chicken soup
1/4 cup diced onion
1 can (5 ounces) chicken

    Cook noodles in water according to package directions and drain.
    In a saucepan, heat soup, onion, chicken, and just under 1/2 of the seasoning packet over medium heat 5 minutes. Top warm noodles with soup mixture.

Chicken with Mushrooms

MAKES 2–4 SERVINGS

1/4 cup butter or margarine
1 pound boneless, skinless chicken tenders, cut into chunks
2 cups sliced fresh mushrooms
2 packages chicken ramen noodles, with seasoning packets

In a frying pan, melt butter and brown chicken until done. Add mushrooms and sauté 5 minutes, or until tender.

Cook noodles in water according to package directions and drain. Add 1 seasoning packet. Top warm noodles with chicken and mushrooms.

51

Chicken Alfredo

MAKES 2 SERVINGS

2 boneless, skinless chicken breasts, cut into strips
2 packages ramen noodles, any flavor
1 cup butter or margarine
1 cup heavy cream
2 cups grated Parmesan cheese
2 tablespoons parsley flakes
1/2 teaspoon salt
pepper

In a frying pan, brown chicken until done.

Cook noodles in water according to package directions and drain.

Heat butter and cream in a small saucepan over low heat until butter melts. Stir in remaining ingredients. Top warm noodles with chicken and sauce.

52

Fajita-Inspired Ramen

MAKES 2 SERVINGS

2 boneless, skinless chicken breasts, cut into strips
1 1/2 cups sliced onion
1 cup sliced red or green bell peppers
2 cups salsa
2 packages ramen noodles, any flavor
1/2 cup sour cream

In a frying pan, brown chicken until done. Add onion, peppers, and salsa and cook over medium heat until vegetables are tender.

Cook noodles in water according to package directions and drain. Serve chicken mixture over warm noodles and top with sour cream.

53

Italian Chicken

MAKES 2 SERVINGS

2 boneless, skinless chicken breasts, cut into chunks
1 cup Italian dressing, divided
2 packages ramen noodles, any flavor

If possible, let chicken marinate overnight in 1/2 cup dressing.

Cook noodles in water according to package directions and drain.

In a frying pan, cook chicken in the dressing until golden brown. Drizzle remaining 1/2 cup dressing on noodles and toss. Top with chicken.

54

Fiesta Chicken

MAKES 2–4 SERVINGS

1 pound boneless, skinless chicken breasts, cut into chunks
olive oil
1/2 cup corn
1/2 cup black beans, drained and rinsed
1/2 cup chopped red bell pepper
2 packages Cajun chicken ramen noodles, with seasoning packets
2 to 3 tablespoons sour cream
2 tablespoons salsa

In a frying pan, brown chicken in olive oil. Add corn, black beans, and pepper. Sauté over low heat until heated through and vegetables are tender.

Cook noodles in water according to package directions and drain. Add seasoning packets. Combine noodles with chicken mixture. Stir in sour cream and salsa.

55

Cheesy Chicken Casserole

MAKES 2 SERVINGS

1/4 cup chopped onion
2 tablespoons butter or margarine
1 can (10.75 ounces) condensed cream of chicken soup
1/2 cup milk
1 package chicken ramen noodles, with seasoning packet
1 cup grated sharp cheddar cheese
1 can (5 ounces) white chicken chunks, drained

Preheat oven to 350 degrees.

In a saucepan, sauté onion in butter until tender. Add soup, milk, and just under 1/2 of the seasoning packet. Stir until smooth.

Cook noodles in water according to package directions and drain. Add cheese, chicken, and soup mixture. Stir until cheese is melted. Pour into a 1-quart greased casserole dish and bake 30 minutes.

56

Chicken 'n' Asparagus

MAKES 4 SERVINGS

4 boneless, skinless chicken breasts
2 packages chicken ramen noodles, with seasoning packets
2 cans (10.75 ounces each) condensed cream of asparagus or mushroom soup
1 cup milk
1/2 pound fresh asparagus, cut up
1 cup grated cheddar cheese

In a frying pan, brown chicken until done. Add noodles, 1 seasoning packet, soup, milk, and asparagus. Simmer over low heat 10 minutes, or until noodles are done. Sprinkle with cheese before serving.

Chinese-Style Ramen

MAKES 2 SERVINGS

1/2 pound boneless, skinless chicken breasts, cut into chunks
1/4 cup water chestnut halves
1/2 cup snow peas
1/3 cup bean sprouts
1/4 cup celery
2 to 3 teaspoons oil
1 package Oriental ramen noodles, with seasoning packet
1 tablespoon soy sauce

In a frying pan, brown chicken until done. Add water chestnuts, snow peas, bean sprouts, celery, and oil. Sauté until vegetables are tender.

Cook noodles in water according to package directions and drain. Add seasoning packet. Spoon vegetables over warm noodles and sprinkle with soy sauce.

58

Chicken Milano

MAKES 2–4 SERVINGS

1 pound boneless, skinless chicken breasts, cut into chunks
2 teaspoons minced garlic
1 tablespoon olive oil
1/2 cup chopped sun-dried tomatoes
1 tablespoon basil
1/2 cup chicken broth
2 packages chicken ramen noodles, with seasoning packets
salt and pepper, to taste

In a frying pan, brown chicken and garlic in oil until done. Add sundried tomatoes, basil, and chicken broth. Simmer over low heat 5 minutes.

Cook noodles in water according to package directions and drain. Add 1 seasoning packet. Serve chicken mixture over warm noodles. Season with salt and pepper.

59–67

PORK

59

All-American Ramen

MAKES 2–4 SERVINGS

2 packages ramen noodles, any flavor, with seasoning packets
1/4 cup chopped onion
4 hot dogs, sliced
1 cup grated cheddar cheese

   Cook noodles in water according to package directions and drain. Add seasoning packets.
   In a frying pan, sauté onion and hot dogs together until heated through. Add hot dog mixture to noodles. Add cheese and stir until melted.

60

Ham and Cheese Ramen Omelets

MAKES 2–4 SERVINGS

2 packages ramen noodles, any flavor, with seasoning packets
2 tablespoons butter or margarine
6 eggs, beaten
1 cup chopped ham
1/2 cup chopped onion
1/2 cup chopped green bell pepper
1/2 to 1 cup grated Swiss cheese

Cook noodles in water according to package directions and drain. Add seasoning packets.

In a frying pan, melt butter, and then add beaten eggs. Fold in noodles and remaining ingredients. Cook until light brown.

61

Cheesy Bacon Noodles

MAKES 2–4 SERVINGS

**2 packages ramen noodles, any flavor
2 cups grated cheddar cheese
1/2 to 1 cup bacon, cooked and crumbled
salt and pepper, to taste**

Cook noodles in water according to package directions and drain. Add cheese immediately and stir until melted. Stir in bacon and season with salt and pepper.

62

Brats 'n' Noodles

MAKES 2–4 SERVINGS

**2 packages ramen noodles, any flavor, with seasoning packets
4 bratwursts or cheddarwursts, sliced**

Boil noodles and brats together. Drain and stir in 1 seasoning packet.

63

Pork and Peppers

MAKES 2 SERVINGS

2 pork chops
1/4 cup chopped red bell pepper
1/4 cup chopped green bell pepper
2 tablespoons chopped onion
1 package pork ramen noodles, with seasoning packet
2 tablespoons butter or margarine
2 tablespoons our
1 cup water mixed with seasoning packet
1 tablespoon vinegar
1/4 teaspoon tarragon leaves
1/4 teaspoon thyme leaves

In a frying pan, brown pork chops until done and then remove. Sauté peppers and onion in drippings until tender.

Cook noodles in water according to package directions and drain.

In a small saucepan, heat butter over low heat until light brown. Add flour, stirring until deep brown. Remove from heat. Add remaining ingredients. Heat to boiling and stir 1 minute. Top warm noodles with pork chops and sauce.

64

Pork Chop Ramen

MAKES 4 SERVINGS

4 pork chops
1 teaspoon oil
1/2 cup sliced onion
1 can (10.75 ounces) condensed cream of celery soup
1/2 cup water
2 packages pork ramen noodles, with seasoning packets

In a frying pan over medium heat, brown pork chops in oil 5 minutes per side, or until done, and drain. Add onion, soup, and water. Simmer over low heat 10 minutes.

Cook noodles in water according to package directions and drain. Add seasoning packets. Serve pork chops and sauce over warm noodles.

65

Hungarian-Style Skillet Meal

MAKES 2 SERVINGS

1 package ramen noodles, any flavor
1/2 pound pork strips
1 can (8 ounces) tomato sauce
1/4 cup onion, thinly sliced
1 teaspoon paprika
1/3 cup sour cream

Cook noodles in water according to package directions and drain.

In a frying pan, brown pork until done. Add tomato sauce, onion, paprika, and noodles. Cook over low heat until onion is tender. Stir in noodles. Remove from heat and add sour cream.

66

Lean Pork Steak

MAKES 2 SERVINGS

2 packages pork ramen noodles, with seasoning packets
2 lean pork steaks, cut into bite-size pieces
1 teaspoon dried minced onion
3/4 cup water

    Cook noodles in water according to package directions and drain.
    In a frying pan, cook steak pieces until done. Add onion, water, and seasoning packets. Simmer, covered, 10 minutes. Stir in noodles and simmer 3–5 minutes more.

67

Tropical Ramen

MAKES 2 SERVINGS

2 packages ramen noodles, any flavor
2 cups cooked ham, cut into strips
1 cup pineapple chunks
1 cup crispy Chinese noodles
1 stalk celery, sliced

Cook noodles in water according to package directions and drain. Rinse with cold water.
Stir in ham, pineapple, crispy noodles, and celery.

68–74

SEAFOOD

68

Cheesy Tuna Ramen

MAKES 2–4 SERVINGS

2 packages ramen noodles, any flavor
2 cans (10.75 ounces each) condensed cream of mushroom soup
1 cup milk
2 cans (5 ounces each) tuna, drained
2 cups peas
2 cups grated cheddar cheese

    Cook noodles in water according to package directions and drain. Add soup, milk, tuna, and peas. Simmer 5 minutes. Sprinkle cheese over top and serve.

69

Tuna Noodle Casserole

MAKES 2–4 SERVINGS

2 cans (5 ounces each) tuna, drained
1 cup grated cheddar cheese
1/2 cup water
1 cup milk
2 eggs, beaten
2 packages chicken ramen noodles, broken up, with seasoning packets
10 to 20 saltine crackers, crushed

Preheat oven to 350 degrees.
In a bowl, mix tuna, cheese, water, milk, eggs, and 1 seasoning packet. Transfer mixture to a casserole dish. Add broken uncooked noodles. Bake 15 minutes, stirring occasionally. Sprinkle crackers over top and bake 5 minutes more.

70

Twice-Baked Tuna Casserole

MAKES 2–4 SERVINGS

**2 packages ramen noodles, any flavor, with seasoning packets
2 cans (5 ounces each) tuna, drained
1 cup cheese
1/2 cup chopped onion
1 cup crushed potato chips**

Preheat oven to 350 degrees.

Cook noodles in water according to package directions and drain. Season with 1 seasoning packet. Mix tuna, cheese, onion, and noodles together in a small casserole dish and bake 15–20 minutes. Sprinkle chips over top and bake 15 minutes more.

71

Creamy Mushroom Shrimp Ramen

MAKES 2 SERVINGS

1 package Oriental ramen noodles, with seasoning packet
1 can (10.75 ounces) condensed cream of mushroom soup
1 can (4 ounces) shrimp, drained
1 cup sliced fresh mushrooms

Cook noodles in water according to package directions; do not drain. Add soup, shrimp, mushrooms, and 1/2 of the seasoning packet. Cook 10 minutes over medium heat.

72

Cheesy Salmon Noodles

MAKES 2 SERVINGS

1 package ramen noodles, any flavor
1 can (10.75 ounces) condensed cream of mushroom soup
1/2 cup milk
1 can (5 ounces) salmon, drained
1 cup cooked spinach or asparagus
1 cup grated cheddar cheese

Cook noodles in water according to package directions and drain. Add soup, milk, salmon, and broccoli. Simmer 5 minutes. Sprinkle cheese over top and serve.

73

Shrimp Ramen

MAKES 2 SERVINGS

1 package Oriental ramen noodles, with seasoning packet
1 can (10.75 ounces) condensed cream of celery soup
1 can (4 ounces) shrimp, drained
salt and pepper, to taste

Cook noodles in water according to package directions and drain. Add just under 1/2 of the seasoning packet. Add soup, shrimp, salt, and pepper. Cook 10 minutes over medium heat.

74

Garlic Shrimp 'n' Veggies

MAKES 2–4 SERVINGS

1 green bell pepper, thinly sliced
1 red bell pepper, thinly sliced
1/2 small onion, thinly sliced
1 1/2 tablespoons minced garlic
3 to 4 tablespoons olive oil
2 cups cooked small shrimp, peeled and deveined
2 packages Oriental ramen noodles, with seasoning packets

In a frying pan, sauté peppers, onion, and garlic in olive oil until tender. Add shrimp and 1 seasoning packet. Simmer 3–5 minutes.

Cook noodles in water according to package directions and drain. Add 1/2 of remaining seasoning packet. Serve shrimp mixture over noodles.

FAMILY FAVORITES

75

Ramen Nachos

MAKES 2 SERVINGS

1 package beef ramen noodles, broken up, with seasoning packet
1/2 cup cubed American cheese
1 cup chili
1 cup crushed corn chips
sour cream
1 green onion, chopped

Cook noodles in water according to package directions and drain. Add 1/2 of the seasoning packet.

In a saucepan, stir warm noodles, cheese, chili, and crushed chips together over low heat until cheese is melted. Garnish with sour cream and green onion.

76

Garlic Noodle Sauté

MAKES 2–4 SERVINGS

2 packages chicken ramen noodles, with seasoning packets
2 cups sliced fresh mushrooms
1/2 red onion, sliced
1 tablespoon minced garlic
olive oil

Cook noodles in water according to package directions and drain. Season with 1 seasoning packet.

In a frying pan, sauté mushrooms, onion, and garlic in olive oil until tender. Add warm noodles and sauté 2 minutes.

Creamy Alfredo Noodles

MAKES 2–3 SERVINGS

**2 packages ramen noodles, any flavor
1 cup butter or margarine
1 cup cream
2 cups freshly grated Parmesan cheese
1 teaspoon garlic salt
Italian seasoning, to taste
pepper, to taste**

Cook noodles in water according to package directions and drain.

In a saucepan, heat butter and cream over low heat until butter is melted. Stir in remaining ingredients. Simmer sauce 5 minutes. Serve over warm noodles.

78

Crunchy, Cheesy Casserole

MAKES 2–4 SERVINGS

2 packages chicken mushroom ramen noodles, with seasoning packets
1 cup cubed Monterey Jack cheese
1/2 cup diced green chilies
1/4 cup sliced black olives
1 cup sour cream
1 cup grated cheddar cheese
1/4 cup grated Parmesan cheese
1/2 cup crushed corn chips

Preheat oven to 400 degrees.
Cook noodles in water according to package directions; rinse with cold water. Combine noodles, seasoning packets, Monterey Jack cheese, chilies, and olives. Stir in sour cream.
Spoon noodle mixture into a greased casserole dish. Sprinkle with remaining cheeses and chips. Bake 20 minutes, or until brown and bubbly.

79

Pizza Pasta

MAKES 2–4 SERVINGS

2 packages ramen noodles, any flavor
2 to 3 cups spaghetti sauce
20 to 25 pepperoni slices, halved
3/4 cup chopped green bell pepper
1/2 cup grated cheddar cheese
1 cup grated mozzarella cheese

Preheat oven to 350 degrees.

Cook noodles in water according to package directions and drain.

In a saucepan, combine sauce, pepperoni, pepper, and cheddar cheese. Stir constantly until cheese is melted.

Place noodles in a lightly greased 8x8-inch pan. Pour sauce mixture over top. Sprinkle with mozzarella cheese. Bake 15 minutes, or until cheese is melted.

80

Lasagna

MAKES 2–4 SERVINGS

2 packages ramen noodles, any flavor
2 cups spaghetti sauce
1 cup ricotta cheese
1 cup grated mozzarella cheese
1 cup Parmesan cheese

Preheat oven to 350 degrees.
Cook noodles in water according to package directions and drain. Stir sauce into noodles.
In an 8x8-inch pan, layer half of the noodle mixture, 1/2 cup ricotta, 1/2 cup mozzarella, and 1/2 cup Parmesan cheeses. Repeat layers. Bake 20 minutes.

81

Meaty Spaghetti

MAKES 2–4 SERVINGS

2 packages ramen noodles, any flavor
1 to 2 cups spaghetti sauce
1 pound ground beef or sausage, browned and drained
grated Parmesan cheese

Cook noodles in water according to package directions and drain.

In a saucepan, heat sauce and cooked beef over medium heat 3–5 minutes, or until heated through. Spoon sauce over warm noodles and then sprinkle with cheese.

82

Primavera Pasta

MAKES 2–4 SERVINGS

1/4 cup slivered almonds
1 cup chopped broccoli
1 cup snow peas
1 cup sliced red bell pepper
1/2 cup thinly sliced carrots
1/2 cup thinly sliced red onion
3 tablespoons vegetable oil
2 packages chicken ramen noodles, broken up
1 1/2 cups water

In a frying pan, toast almonds until lightly browned, and then set aside. Stir-fry vegetables in oil 3–4 minutes. Add broken noodles and water. Steam 3–5 minutes, or until noodles are done, stirring occasionally. Top with toasted almonds to serve.

83

Parmesan Noodles

MAKES 2–4 SERVINGS

**2 packages ramen noodles, any flavor
1/2 cup grated Parmesan cheese
salt and pepper, to taste**

Cook noodles in water according to package directions and drain. Add Parmesan to warm noodles and stir until cheese is melted. Sprinkle with more Parmesan cheese if desired. Season with salt and pepper.

84

Cheesy Noodles

MAKES 2–4 SERVINGS

2 packages ramen noodles, any flavor
1 cup cubed American processed cheese
1/2 to 3/4 cup milk
salt and pepper, to taste

    Cook noodles in water according to package directions and drain. Add cheese and milk and stir until cheese is melted. Season with salt and pepper.

85

Cheesy Ranch Ramen

MAKES 2–4 SERVINGS

2 packages finely chopped ramen noodles, any flavor
1 cup ranch dressing
2 cups grated cheddar cheese

Cook noodles in water according to package directions and drain. Add ranch dressing and cheese to noodles and cook over low heat, stirring constantly, until cheese is melted.

86

Buttery Chive Noodles

MAKES 2–4 SERVINGS

**2 packages ramen noodles, any flavor
2 tablespoons butter or margarine
1/2 cup chopped chives
salt and pepper, to taste**

Cook noodles in water according to package directions and drain. Add butter to warm noodles and stir until melted. Add chives and season with salt and pepper.

87

Onion Noodles

MAKES 2 SERVINGS

2 tablespoons vegetable oil
1 package ramen noodles, any flavor, broken up
1 can (10.75 ounces) condensed onion soup
1 soup can water
1 to 2 tablespoons chopped chives

Heat oil in a saucepan over medium heat. Add noodles and lightly brown, stirring constantly. Add soup and water. Cover and simmer 10 minutes. Drain noodles and serve with chives sprinkled over top.

88

Ramen Trail Mix

MAKES 12 CUPS

3 packages ramen noodles, any flavor
15 small sticks beef jerky, cut into small pieces
1/2 pound dried apricots or other dried fruit, cut into small pieces
1/2 cup dried cranberries, blueberries, cherries, or bananas
2 cups dry roasted peanuts

Break noodles into a bowl. Add remaining ingredients and stir.

For a more traditional trail mix, omit the beef jerky and fruit. Add 1 pound plain M&Ms, 1 cup raisins, 1 cup sunflower seeds, and 3 cups granola cereal to broken-up noodles and stir.

89

Ramen Haystacks

MAKES 4–6 SERVINGS

2 cups butterscotch chips
1 tablespoon butter
1 tablespoon milk
1 package ramen noodles, any flavor, crumbled

In a saucepan, heat butterscotch, butter, and milk over low heat until chips are completely melted. Stir crumbled, uncooked noodles into butterscotch mixture until coated. Place spoon-size balls on wax paper, and refrigerate until cool.

90

Crunchy Chocolate-Coconut Bars

MAKES 6–8 SERVINGS

2 packages ramen noodles, any flavor
3 cups milk chocolate chips
2 cups mini marshmallows
1/2 cup coconut
1/2 cup chopped walnuts

Preheat oven to 350 degrees.
Do not break noodles. Put blocks of noodles in a lightly greased 8x8-inch pan. Cover with layers of chocolate chips and marshmallows. Heat in warm oven until marshmallows and chocolate chips are melted. Layer remaining ingredients over top and refrigerate. When cooled, cut into bars.

91

Peach Treats

MAKES 2 SERVINGS

1 cup cream
1 can (8.5 ounces) peaches, drained with juice reserved
1/4 cup brown sugar
1 package ramen noodles, any flavor, crushed
1/2 cup crushed Frosted Flakes

Preheat oven to 350 degrees.
In a small casserole dish, mix cream, peaches and 1/2 cup of their juices, and brown sugar. Add crushed noodles, making sure they are completely covered by cream mixture. Bake 5 minutes. Sprinkle Frosted Flakes over top and bake 5 minutes more.

92

Maple and Brown Sugar Ramenmeal

MAKES 2 SERVINGS

- **1 package ramen noodles, any flavor**
- **1 cup milk**
- **1 tablespoon maple syrup**
- **1 tablespoon brown sugar**

Crumble ramen into a microwave-safe bowl. Pour in milk, syrup, and brown sugar. Microwave on high 4 minutes, stirring occasionally.

If you'd rather have something fruity, omit the syrup and sugar and add 1 sliced banana, 1 cup blueberries, or a mixture of 1/2 diced apples, 1 teaspoon cinnamon, and 1 tablespoon sugar.

VEGETABLE ENTRÉES

93

Broccoli-Cauliflower Ramen

MAKES 2 SERVINGS

1 can (10.75 ounces) condensed cream of celery soup
1/2 cup milk
1 cup broccoli pieces
1/2 cup cauliflower pieces
1/2 cup sliced carrots
1 package ramen noodles, any flavor, with seasoning packet

In a saucepan, heat soup and milk to boiling. Stir in vegetables and heat to boiling. Reduce heat and simmer 15 minutes.

Cook noodles in water according to package directions and drain. Add seasoning packet. Top warm noodles with soup mixture.

94

Cheesy Vegetable Ramen

MAKES 2 SERVINGS

1 package ramen noodles, any flavor, with seasoning packet
1 cup frozen mixed vegetables
1 tablespoon water
1 small jar creamy cheese sauce, condensed

Cook noodles in water according to package directions and drain. Add 1/2 of the seasoning packet and set aside.

In a frying pan, cook vegetables in water until tender. Add cheese sauce to vegetables and heat through. Stir in noodles.

95

Hollandaise Vegetable Noodles

MAKES 2 SERVINGS

1 package chicken ramen noodles, with seasoning packet
2 egg yolks
3 tablespoons lemon juice
1/2 cup butter or margarine
1 cup fresh or frozen mixed vegetables

Cook noodles in water according to package directions and drain.

In a saucepan, whisk egg yolks and lemon juice briskly with a fork. Add 1/2 of the butter and stir over low heat until melted. Add remaining butter, stirring briskly until melted and sauce thickens. Cook vegetables and drain. Top warm noodles with vegetables and sauce.

96

Veggie Sauté

MAKES 2 SERVINGS

1 package ramen noodles, any flavor, with seasoning packet
1/2 cup sliced onion
1/2 cup diced tomato
1 can (4 ounces) mushrooms, drained
1/2 cup chopped green bell pepper
1 teaspoon garlic powder
2 tablespoons oil

Cook noodles in water according to package directions and drain. Season noodles with 1/2 of the seasoning packet.

In a frying pan, sauté vegetables in garlic powder and oil over low heat until tender. Stir in warm noodles.

97

Chinese-Style Fried Noodles

MAKES 2–4 SERVINGS

2 packages Oriental ramen noodles, with seasoning packets
1 cup frozen peas and carrots
2 eggs
1 to 2 teaspoons oil
2 to 3 tablespoons soy sauce

Cook noodles in water according to package directions and drain. Add seasoning packets. Heat vegetables in microwave until heated through and add to warm noodles.

In a frying pan, fry eggs in oil; break yolk and cook until hard, flipping occasionally. Cut eggs into small pieces. Stir into noodle mixture. Sprinkle soy sauce over top and stir together, adding more if necessary.

98

Tomato Sauté

MAKES 2–4 SERVINGS

2 packages ramen noodles, any flavor, with seasoning packets
1 cup butter or margarine
2 cans (14.5 ounces each) diced tomatoes
2 teaspoons minced garlic
salt and pepper, to taste

Cook noodles in water according to package directions and drain.

In a frying pan, melt butter. Add tomatoes, garlic, seasoning packets, and noodles and stir. Season with salt and pepper. Simmer 5 minutes.

99

Garlic and Cilantro Noodles

MAKES 2–4 SERVINGS

2 packages Oriental ramen noodles, with seasoning packets
2 cups fresh or frozen mixed vegetables
1 teaspoon minced garlic
2 tablespoons fresh chopped cilantro

Cook noodles and mixed vegetables in water together and drain. Add garlic, cilantro, and seasoning packets. Simmer over low heat 5 minutes, stirring occasionally.

100

Creamy Corn and Cheese Noodles

MAKES 2 SERVINGS

1 package ramen noodles, any flavor, with seasoning packet
1 1/2 cups grated cheddar cheese
1 can (14 ounces) creamed corn

Cook noodles in water according to package directions and drain. Add seasoning packet.

In a saucepan, heat cheese and corn over medium heat, stirring occasionally, until the cheese is melted. Mix with warm noodles.

Soy Sauce Veggie Noodles

MAKES 2 SERVINGS

1 package Oriental ramen noodles, with seasoning packet
1 cup frozen stir-fry vegetables
1 1/2 teaspoons olive oil
1 tablespoon soy sauce
salt and pepper, to taste

Cook noodles in water according to package directions and drain. Add seasoning packet.

In a frying pan, sauté vegetables in olive oil until heated through, then add to warm noodles. Sprinkle soy sauce over top and stir together. Season with salt and pepper.

Metric Conversion Chart

VOLUME MEASUREMENTS		WEIGHT MEASUREMENTS		TEMPERATURE CONVERSION	
U.S.	Metric	U.S.	Metric	Fahrenheit	Celsius
1 teaspoon	5 ml	1/2 ounce	15 g	250	120
1 tablespoon	15 ml	1 ounce	30 g	300	150
1/4 cup	60 ml	3 ounces	90 g	325	160
1/3 cup	75 ml	4 ounces	115 g	350	180
1/2 cup	125 ml	8 ounces	225 g	375	190
2/3 cup	150 ml	12 ounces	350 g	400	200
3/4 cup	175 ml	1 pound	450 g	425	220
1 cup	250 ml	2 1/4 pounds	1 kg	450	230

MORE 101 THINGS® IN THESE FAVORITES

BACON
CAKE MIX
CASSEROLE
SLOW COOKER
SMOKER

Available at bookstores or directly from Gibbs Smith
1.800.835.4993
www.gibbs-smith.com
Ebooks available through your favorite digital retailer

About the Author

Toni Patrick is the culinary creative behind the wildly successful *101 Things to Do With Ramen Noodles*, as well as several other titles in the popular 101 Things® series, including *101 Things to Do With Mac & Cheese* and *101 More Things to Do With Ramen Noodles*. She has been featured on the Food Network and lives in Greeley, Colorado.

www.ingramcontent.com/pod-product-compliance
Lightning Source LLC
Chambersburg PA
CBHW011956150426
43200CB00017B/2922